Traveling Far and Home

poems by

Jessie Schira

Finishing Line Press
Georgetown, Kentucky

Traveling Far and Home

ACKNOWLEDGMENTS

Special thanks go out to my longtime friend, Cara, who loves stories as much
as I do, and thankfully loves to edit.
More thanks to my mother, father and sister. Without their stories, and
dreams, I would not have had the courage to share my own.
And to my husband, Tyler, for many more things than I have words to
describe.

Editor: Christen Kincaid

Cover Art: Jackie Schira

Author Photo: Jackie Schira

Cover Design: Elizabeth Maines

Printed in the USA on acid-free paper.
Order online: www.finishinglinepress.com
                also available on amazon.com

Author inquiries and mail orders:
Finishing Line Press
P. O. Box 1626
Georgetown, Kentucky 40324
U. S. A.

Table of Contents

Fishing 1

My grandfather. 1963. Fish Creek. 4

Lake Michigan. April. 5

Whitefish Dunes. 6

The pond. August. 7

There are leaves 8

I do not know what 9

Berothal. Point Beach. March. 10

Warmth. 12

Sheboygan. 13

Burrowing 14

Pliable 15

If I should ever return. 16

For Grandma Schira

Fishing.

Eh it's 3 am and I am wondering why I agreed to this trip,
and then I am on the water being willed to remember.
There it is.
The chill of the air as they push that throttle down,
the bow of the Pro-line pulling up into the air.
Oh! And the splash of water
the lake shares with me
as the boat smacks
against the challenging waves.
The choppy, but not too choppy, lake
that might as well be an ocean,
is running in front of me,
we try to catch up to that rising sun.
The gold crossing the fluid plains
is the only source of warmth,
but I'm pretty sure it is in my head.
And then we are trolling,
waiting for fish to be
hungry or anxious or bored.
My Dramamine choosing not to work
and my greasy egg sandwich
threatening to make me taste it twice.
I beg my stomach
not to add to the froth around the boat.
But it does and I am handed a cold beer to
clean the buds.
Thankfully my uncle bought anything but the
skunky Corona my dad drinks.
We are waiting for that first nab.
To be the first that morning in the myriad of fishers,
 fumbling around for a flashlight.

So my dad starts telling stories about all the times
he sank boats out here and
dropped engines into the water that
grandpa made him go get,
twenty feet deep into the dank mud.
And I hear about the time Doc's sailboat
threw my dad off the deck and
he watched the boat go by
so his crew could win the race.
And I hear about the Christmas Tree Ship
and how it sank before it could deliver those trees.
Grandma had painted that story several times.
Then there are the times my dad drank too much beer
and had to sleep on the dock.
The times when my grandmother's best friend
was the first female millionaire,
whose yacht was next to theirs.
A yacht that disappeared
when the money disappeared;
when children needed guidance,
not money, or drugs.
He moved on to a simple farming life
far away from the marina.
And I am reminded of all the times
my grandpa was a great man.
Like the times he took my dad
down to the lake and taught him how to fly fish.
Like all the times my dad took me
down to the lake.
Then the line jumps
and we jump higher, reeling it in.

Only a little.
Don't horse it.
The fish runs a little like the
shark in *Jaws*
but our boat won't follow.
This one is putting up a fight.
And then my dad is smiling,
because I reigned in that monster eight inch.
Wait. I mean eighteen inch salmon.
There it is.
The slimy smell of the fish as I pull it off the line.
And the sickening feeling as
I needle the hook with a twist and turn.
And we are posing for that picture
and I am holding that fish
way out in front of me,
my arms extended
because that's the way we do it.

My grandfather. 1963. Fish Creek.

The Lake is quiet today.
The sky, dull.
An abundant fog suspends above the water.
A man stands at the end of the dock, fishing.
Dark blue boat shoes,
holed jeans, short-sleeved flannel.
A long goose neck,
cherry wood, snake-scaled print
tobacco pipe hangs from his mouth.
Red, white, blue stars—his coffee cup.
Cold, half-sugar, half-coffee flavored water.
Slow surfs filter
onto the pebbled beach.
A gentle voice rolls out
inaccessible sounds of solitude.
The perch are reeled in,
released, reeled in.
Founder's Square is filled
with laughter.
Kids chasing bats in the attic of Fish Creek Inn,
catch, release.

Lake Michigan. April.

Is it cold, I ask. Nah, he says.
I should have noticed the eagerness in my father's voice.
My leap from the small bow of Bud's Dory
was rewarded with the
brusque language of the lake.
Biting, provoking, penetrating.
I gasp.
Water laughs its way into my lungs.
My chest is put on ice,
choking my desire to scream.
My skin tries to adapt—
Numbness.
The water is no longer winning.

Whitefish Dunes.

The silver-white skies
our brilliant eyes settle on.
I expect something more.
A bite of breeze,
a nibble of sea
on sand below
my feet,
or is it the tug
of the moon
pulling me to you
that startles me?

The pond. August.

Blackberries hang,
gentle not to knock the branch
for fear they will fall
into the thorned abyss below.

An abandoned raft
on a graveled island,
made with old grey posts
from ginseng gardens.

A pink paddleboat,
turtles bathing on its seats
their eggs resting in soupy mud
where human feet once rested.

The neglected bridge
a son built for his father,
collapsed, but still striving
to connect to that fishing spot.

A raggedy red shack
a young couple dreamed
of living in, with
no plumbing, no water, candlelight.

There are leaves

There are leaves
peeking from beneath
a heavy snow.
Yellow patches
of scared foliage.
Old black maple
stands bare,
bold brown branches
fight with the wind.
A family of grey squirrels
betting on the tree,
missing the leaves.

I do not know what

I do not know what
it is about you
that I cannot hold

Is it the tender smell of your nape
the internal burgeoning
of your crisp violet heart

The rhythm of your impression
strides amongst my freckles
confidently stepping to the colors
of my swirl of hair

Why do I seek
the stream of your marrow
the gentle rotundity of your lips
lashes that spread out your sincerity

Warmth from the wings
a budding bird ripples
in a stir of plumage
moves my devotion to sit
beside your own

Betrothal. Point Beach. March.

White-tipped waves lull me,
Rouse us.

Let's go camping.
Point beach, he responded.

The hilltop sheds its forested greens.
Pale sand crumbles beneath my feet.
Spots of shrub
Poke their way through
The beach ahead—vacant.

You run ahead.
I follow.

Clammy hands,
take my chilled fingers.
I turn.
My cheeks—brushed by
March-driven wind and mists.

The lake
is telling me that
he is saying something to me.

Pay attention.

Instead, we fell to the sands,
wasting the carefully planned words.

Creamy sand
seeping into your hair.
Whispering waves
ripple glad wishes.

Your eyes match the lake,
mostly green, lulling me in, tearing at my yes.

I am waiting to see,
what these wild winds will bring.

Warmth

Warmth of the sun on ray-bleached fingers.
Wind on freckles.
Yellow birds wane on petals
—dancing to the breeze.
Water dribbles from the leaves,
in fond remembrance—
tender caresses.
Seeds for tomorrow
sprinkled on the wind
laid to rest in the soil
dug by today's firm hands.
Eyes that wander the sky willing, wanting, praying
are caught in strange wonder.
To be taken with high regard
the beauty of smaller sights.

Sheboygan.

look at that wave, that water, that rock. i love, i love, i
see it growing, growing till it tumbles over into a
castle of foam. oh, love. Soft, sweet love, tickle me
till my toes numb and hair curls. my mind lulls to a
sleep, and my heart thinks in its place.

Burrowing

Burrowing deep into
drying lake bottom
surviving or am I being stimulated?
I take up the challenge
to move through the mire,
and throw my luck
into the rivulet that carried my
dreams like sea plants
stretching, thriving, catching
golden ray-strands.
Bent that way, curved this way
like rivers,
meandering into questions
or rain drops in oceans
mixing with salt,
mixing with the traffic of
seabirds and sea raiders.
Challenging to reach the mud,
The muck,
The answers.
I am trekking through that
primordial soup and it
gooeys beneath my
red-tipped toes.
And my cat lays there humming his happiness
looking at me with his I-might-eat-you-later eyes.
And what we do, will echo eternity through.
And I am not sure if I have lost my way.

pliable

tonight i can say
       hello pretty
hello there.
i see you.
i see the leaves. it's that green plant. that pretty Jade life. and
i've been wondering how you get that budding desire. that
Lush developing youth.
Please.
no obscurities.
are you so callow? so new that you do not know where you
should go?

tonight i say
life has a mustache and holds a pipe between his teeth. he
wants to tell you his story. he wants to share his wisdom. it is

time sits on the wall watching the fuzz float around the room.
caught in their eddy. their paces. time will

wait

your interim is up.

If I should ever return,

If I should ever return,
I would see that we grew up there.
We plundered the blackberry bushes,
a bloody battle of thorns
—a sweet, but bloody battle.
A quick dart up the hill,
a dodge through thorns,
snatched berries in an
ice cream bucket
—half the berries surviving the journey.
We slept in the trees,
the oak, the elms,
the ratty old pine filled with ants.
We licked sticky maple from our fingers,
and ate the bitter apples from the twisted apple tree.
I would see that we lived in the garden.
Where we pounded in the posts,
and strung the old metal fencing.
Rows of beans, peas, peppers, and tomatoes
marked by jagged quartz.

A back pocket held our time.
And the land held our memories.

A nature enthusiast, **Jessie Schira** is an avid fisher, hiker, and traveler. Though she will always be a Wisconsin girl at heart she currently lives in Minneapolis, Minnesota, with her husband, border collie and their ferocious guard cat.